Helicopters
High-Flying Heroes

Karen and Glen Bledsoe

Enslow Publishers, Inc.
40 Industrial Road
Box 398
Berkeley Heights, NJ 07922
USA

http://www.enslow.com

Library of Congress Cataloging-in-Publication Data

Bledsoe, Karen E.
  Helicopters : high-flying heroes / by Karen and Glen Bledsoe.
      p. cm. — (Mighty military machines)
  Includes bibliographical references and index.
  ISBN 0-7660-2663-9
  1. Military helicopters—Juvenile literature. I. Bledsoe, Glen. II. Title.
III. Series.
  UG1230.B58 2006
  358.4'183—dc22

                                        2006010906

Printed in the United States of America

10 9 8 7 6 5 4 3 2 1

To Our Readers:
We have done our best to make sure all Internet Addresses in this book were active and appropriate when we went to press. However, the author and the publisher have no control over and assume no liability for the material available on those Internet sites or on other Web sites they may link to. Any comments or suggestions can be sent by e-mail to comments@enslow.com or to the address on the back cover.

Photo Credits: Associated Press, AP, p. 14; Department of Defense, pp. 1, 3, 8, 16, 17, 19, 20, 21, 22, 25, 28, 30, 34, 35, 36, 37, 46, 47; Getty Images, pp. 4, 18, 32; Getty Images/Time & Life Pictures, p. 15; U.S. Air Force, pp. 3, 7, 10-11, 12, 26, 31, 40, 41, 42, 46; U.S. Marine Corps, pp. 38, 44.

Cover Photos: Department of Defense

Contents

Chapter ONE

Transport Attack

Staff Sergeant Lance Albert of the Nevada Army National Guard was not expecting a battle that June evening in 2005. Combined U.S. and Afghan troops had been busy fighting opposing soldiers on rocky hillsides northeast of the city of Kandahar, Afghanistan. But by that evening, the fighting had died down.

Albert was part of the crew of a CH-47 Chinook transport helicopter, which was bringing fresh troops to the area. Three attack helicopters, including two

UH-60 Black Hawks, flew alongside the Chinook to protect it. The Chinook landed safely and dropped off the troops. The big transport helicopter lifted off again, with its rear ramp still open. Just as it rose up over a ridge, opposing troops opened fire, aiming straight at the Chinook.

The nose of the big helicopter tilted downward as opposing fire ripped through its metal skin. Albert heard explosions just behind the aircraft, and felt something whiz past his head. A bullet had missed him by only eight inches.

Opposing fire ripped through the helicopter's metal skin.

Another bullet hit one of the Chinook's fuel lines. Fuel sprayed out, soaking Albert's flight suit as well as some of the helicopter's insulation, which had been torn loose in the attack. The insulation smoldered for a few moments, then Albert spotted the first flames shooting out.

"If that goes up [in flames]," Albert thought, "we're all going down like a toasted marshmallow."

The helicopter flew off, moving low and fast. The pilot rocked the aircraft back and forth hard to avoid opposing fire, a move that Albert later called "an extreme yank and bank." But the turning rotors that moved the helicopter through the air also acted like a giant fan, blowing air into the helicopter. This caused the flames to shoot up.

The situation was dangerous, but Albert knew how to handle fire. He had spent several summers working on fire crews, fighting forest fires in Oregon. Even though his flight suit was soaked with fuel, Albert did not hesitate. He grabbed the firefighting equipment on board, including fire extinguishers and a large bucket of water, and doused the flames.

A few minutes later, the pilot set the Chinook down in a wheat field. The whole crew scrambled out, then checked the aircraft to make sure that there were no other fires on board. A Downed Aircraft Recovery Team (DART) flew in on another Chinook to help them patch the damaged fuel lines.

Eight hours later, the damaged Chinook took to the air again. It flew back to its base, where fire crews were waiting in case of another emergency. But the patches to the fuel lines held, and the Chinook landed safely.

Types of Military Helicopters

The CH-47 Chinook transport helicopter that Staff Sergeant Albert rode in is just one kind of military helicopter. Helicopters are used by all branches of the military for combat missions and for rescue. Attack helicopters are armed with high-powered weapons such as machine guns and missiles (rockets carrying explosives that may be launched by remote

FACTFILE

DART: Downed Aircraft Recovery Team

If something goes wrong on a military helicopter while flying in a war zone, the pilot may make an emergency landing wherever he or she can. Often it is far from any road and far from help. If the pilot cannot make the necessary repairs to get into the air again, a Downed Aircraft Recovery Team (DART) may be sent in to help.

A DART crew is usually made up of sixteen trained mechanics aboard a Chinook helicopter. When an emergency call comes in, the crew flies out to find the downed aircraft. Part of the crew makes quick repairs. Other crew members stand guard in case of attack. If the DART can get the helicopter in the air again, they will escort it back to an air base. If they cannot fix the helicopter, the crew may use their Chinook to carry it back to the base. At the base, larger repair crews will take over and fix the helicopter.

control). These weapons are used in battle to attack targets on the ground. Large transport helicopters, like the Chinook, are used for moving soldiers and cargo from one place to another. They may move tanks and other military vehicles as well as large numbers of troops. Smaller transport helicopters are used to move weapons, food, medical equipment, and smaller numbers of troops. They may also rescue

▼ A Coast Guard officer searches for survivors of Hurricane Katrina in New Orleans in 2005. He is flying in an HH-60 Jayhawk helicopter.

downed jet pilots or troops who are trapped by opposing forces.

Different branches of the military use different models of helicopters suited to the missions they perform. The U.S. Army, Navy, Air Force, and Marines all use light transport, heavy transport, and attack helicopters, although each branch uses different models. The U.S. Coast Guard uses transport helicopters for search-and-rescue operations and for finding and stopping smugglers, or people trying to sneak goods into or out of the United States.

Smaller transport helicopters can be used to rescue downed jet pilots.

Military helicopters may also be used to rescue civilians, or nonmilitary citizens. The U.S. Coast Guard and the Navy use helicopters to rescue boaters in distress. Army, Air Force, or National Guard helicopters may be called in to help rescue injured hikers or mountain climbers.

During natural disasters, helicopters may be used to help rescue people and move them away from the disaster zone. When Hurricane Katrina struck New Orleans in August 2005, the Navy, the Coast Guard, and the National Guard responded immediately by sending in helicopters to rescue people who were trapped in the flooded city. Before the disaster was over, all branches of the military responded with helicopters and other rescue vehicles.

Parts of a Helicopter

Every model of helicopter differs from others. But all helicopters have certain parts in common.

Main rotor: The set of blades on the top of a helicopter. As they spin like the blades on an electric fan, they generate lift to help the helicopter into the air. All helicopters have at least one set of rotors. Some have two, stacked on top of each other, that spin in opposite directions. Some have two separate rotors, located one in front of the other. The main rotor is horizontal (parallel to the ground).

Front fuselage

Engine: Sits at the top of a helicopter, just beneath the main rotor. It provides power to the helicopter, making the rotors spin and providing electricity for the various systems on board.

Front fuselage: Part of the body of the aircraft that contains the cockpit, which is where the pilot sits, and where the helicopter's controls are.

Main fuselage: The space inside a helicopter where passengers or cargo may be carried. Also called the cabin.

Tail boom: The part of the helicopter extending out behind the cabin, on which the tail rotor is mounted.

Tail rotor: A vertical (perpendicular to the ground) rotor at the end of the tail boom. This rotor holds the helicopter's body straight in the air. The tail rotor can also help steer the aircraft by moving the tail boom.

Main rotor

Tail rotor

Engine

Tail boom

Main fuselage

Wheels

Wheels

Skids, floats, or wheels: The gear that supports the helicopter when it lands. The type of gear depends on the type of helicopter and where it is expected to land. Skids are useful on soft or uneven ground. Floats are for water landings. Wheels work well on solid ground, where the helicopter may have to move across the ground.

Chapter TWO

Military Helicopters

Though helicopters are important to today's military operations, the military helicopter did not appear until several decades after the invention of the airplane. Helicopters were harder to engineer than airplanes. Designers worked many years trying to solve the problems of helicopter flight.

Igor Sikorsky's Helicopters

People began experimenting with helicopter flight at the beginning of the twentieth century, but the first helicopter that was actually able to fly was built by Raúl Pateras de Pescara of Argentina in 1916. In 1934,

German engineers built the first helicopter whose movement could be controlled by the pilot. These were only single models. No one was producing large numbers of helicopters. In the United States, Russian-born Igor Sikorsky would change that.

In 1939, Sikorsky built the VS-300, which lifted a few feet into the air and was fully controllable. Because of his success, Sikorsky sought out military contracts to build bigger and better helicopters. In 1943, he put a new model, the R-4, into production for military use.

The United States had been involved in World War II (1939–1945) since 1941. The Sikorsky R-4 helicopter proved useful in searching for submarines and looking for opposing troops. In 1945, helicopters lifted seventy wounded soldiers from a battle on Luzon, an island in the Philippines, to field hospitals. This was the first time that helicopters were used near a battle.

In 1945, helicopters lifted seventy wounded soldiers from a battle in the Philippines.

Helicopters were also used in the Korean War (1950–1953) to transport wounded soldiers to field hospitals. By then, other companies, such as Bell Aircraft, were building military helicopters. It was during this time that the helicopter got the

▲ Igor Sikorsky tests one of his early helicopter models in 1941, which set a new record for time in the air. Later, his R-4 would be the first military helicopter.

nickname of "chopper," from the "chop-chop" sound made by the turning rotors.

The United States used military helicopters widely during the Vietnam War, from 1965 to 1973. Thousands of helicopters were used to move troops into battle, and to fly wounded soldiers to hospitals. Most of these were the Bell UH-1 helicopter, nicknamed the "Huey." Helicopters were also armed with machine guns so that they could fly over targets and fire at them. These were the first attack helicopters.

Modern Military Helicopters

Modern helicopters have many improvements over the first military helicopters. They use onboard

A UH-1 helicopter lifts off in Vietnam in 1967. Soldiers protect ▼ themselves from the "wash" kicked up by its spinning rotors.

How Helicopters Fly

A helicopter has at least one horizontal rotor that lifts it off the ground. It also has a second rotor, either horizontal or vertical, located on the tail, that keeps the craft from spinning with the rotor. The second rotor also helps steer the craft by moving the tail. Inside the cockpit, the pilot uses rudder pedals on the floor to control the tail movement.

Helicopters use some of the same principles of flight as airplanes do. Airplanes must move forward at high speeds to get enough air moving downward off the wings to generate lift. Lift is the force that raises an aircraft off the ground. A helicopter's rotor blades are shaped like long, thin wings. Rather than moving forward to generate lift, an engine turns the main rotor at high speed, forcing air downward. This allows helicopters to lift nearly straight off the ground. Because the helicopter needs no forward motion to generate lift, it can hover in one place.

Helicopters also move forward, backward, and to the side by slightly tilting the rotors. This allows the air coming off of the rotor to push both down and slightly backward, forward, or sideways. To do this, the pilot uses control sticks, or levers. The pilot also moves the levers to increase the angle of the rotor blades, allowing the helicopter to climb or descend.

navigation systems that help pilots find their way in the air. They carry radio equipment to communicate with other aircraft and with personnel on the ground. Many helicopters have radar warning systems that warn of approaching missiles.

Military helicopters may also carry weapons. The kind of weapons they carry depends on the type of helicopter. Transport helicopters are often armed with machine guns which they use mostly for defense. Attack helicopters carry machine guns, but are also armed with missile launchers.

The size of a helicopter's crew also depends on the helicopter. Large Chinook transport helicopters have a crew of three or more. The pilot and co-pilot

A soldier checks the rockets loaded into a launcher on an ▼ AH-64 Apache. Attack helicopters like the Apache are the most heavily armed of all helicopters.

fly the helicopter. The flight engineer checks the helicopter before and after each flight, and keeps track of all systems during the flight. Chinooks may carry other crew members who assist with special missions.

Small transport helicopters usually have a crew of four, including a pilot, co-pilot, and one or more crew chiefs who carry out the work of the mission. They may also carry a gunner who controls and fires the weapons. Small attack helicopters usually carry a crew of only two: the pilot and the co-pilot.

▼ Crew members can be seen aboard an HH-60G Pave Hawk as it flies over Iraq in 2003.

Helicopters in the Sand

Every time a helicopter takes off or lands, the rotors kick up loose dust and dirt. But pilots landing helicopters in the deserts of the Middle East face a special challenge. In the desert, countless grains of loose sand can be whipped up by swirling helicopter rotors, forming a dense cloud.

Helicopters lift off the ground and hover in the air when their rotors force air downward. As long as the helicopter is moving forward, the flowing sand, called "wash," is not a problem. This is because the helicopter stays ahead of the blinding cloud of sand. When a helicopter lands, however, it is not moving forward and is surrounded by the wash. Pilots landing in the desert learn to land by "feel" since they are not able to see exactly where they are setting down. In addition to checking instruments, the pilot also brings the aircraft down slowly enough that the pilot's own body senses the landing as a gentle bump.

Chapter THREE

Attack Helicopters

On April 10, 2004, Chief Warrant Officer 2 Marc Macaspac was "driving to work" as he likes to call it. He is a helicopter pilot and was part of a team of two OH-58 Kiowa Warrior helicopters serving in Iraq. They live at one base and fly to work at another.

On that afternoon, Macaspac's usual commute was interrupted by an urgent radio call. A U.S. Army convoy, or group of military vehicles, was under attack. One of the U.S. soldiers had been hit, and a rocket-propelled grenade (RPG) had hit a Humvee (a military vehicle).

The two Kiowa Warrior helicopters flew to the area where the convoy was. As they arrived, they saw soldiers and civilians running to avoid opposing fire. But the helicopter crews could not tell where the fire was coming from. The Kiowa team used their radios to contact the soldiers on the ground and asked them to mark their positions with red smoke. That way, if the helicopter crews saw rifle fire coming from an area without red smoke, they would know where the opposing fighters were hidden.

As they scouted the area to find out where the opposing fire was coming from, the pilots flew their Kiowas under power lines and between trees. They needed to fly low so that they could spot the fighters, but fast so they would be difficult to shoot at.

A Humvee leads a convoy of tractor trailers. Convoys bring ▼ tons of supplies to soldiers fighting in Iraq. Sometimes attack helicopters are called in to defend convoys.

As they flew near the convoy, Macaspac saw that the U.S. soldiers were shooting into a line of trees. He and his team flew into the trees to investigate.

Just beyond the edge of the trees, Macaspac spotted a group of about five men crouching in a pit, all dressed in black and holding AK-47 assault rifles. The Kiowa helicopters were no more than twenty-five feet from the men in the pit. Macaspac told his team to keep flying and let the men in the pit think that they had not been spotted. The helicopters flew on for another half mile, then turned back. Macaspac's co-pilot fired their machine gun, but it jammed. Thinking quickly, Macaspac flew the helicopter up over the trees, and fired his M-4 rifle into the pit.

Macaspac's team had rockets, but they were difficult to fire straight down. So Macaspac moved the helicopter directly above, pointed its nose down, and

FACTFILE

Kiowa Warrior Fact Sheet

Primary use: Attack helicopter
Height: 12 feet, 10 inches
Width: 6 feet, 5 inches
Length: 33 feet, 4 inches
Rotor diameter: 35 feet
Maximum speed: 128 mph
Crew members: Pilot, co-pilot
Weapons: Rocket launchers, machine guns, missile launchers

fired the rockets. Meanwhile, the second Kiowa Warrior came up with its machine gun firing. Together, the two helicopters cleared the area. U.S. soldiers soon discovered that the men in the pit had been the only ones firing on the convoy. The battle was over.

Chief Warrant Officer 2 Marc Macaspac and Chief Warrant Officer 2 Eric Bushmaker, the pilot of the second helicopter, received the Air Medal with Valor Device for their heroism and bravery.

What Is an Attack Helicopter?

Attack helicopters are light, two-seat, single-rotor aircraft that are designed to attack ground forces. They are armored, and carry weapons and sensors to seek, attack, and destroy targets. Depending on the helicopter, its weapons, and its mission, the targets may include armored vehicles, buildings, troops, ships, or submarines. There are many kinds of attack helicopters. They include the OH-58D Kiowa Warrior and the AH-64 Apache used by the U.S. Army, the U.S Navy's SH-2 Sea Sprite, and the AH-1 Cobra, used by the U.S. Marines. The U.S. Coast Guard's MH-64A Stingray is an interdiction helicopter. Armed like an attack helicopter, its mission is to stop smugglers and dangerous watercraft.

Attack helicopters usually carry a two-person crew of pilot and co-pilot. The pilot flies the helicopter. The co-pilot helps navigate, or direct where they are going, and helps fly the helicopter when needed. The co-pilot also fills the role of gunner, firing weapons while the pilot keeps the helicopter moving.

Attack helicopters are among the fastest helicopters. The AH-64 Apache can fly as fast as 225 miles per hour (mph). Some, such as the Apache, are designed to fly during daylight hours. Others, such as the Kiowa Warrior, are designed mostly for night flight. They carry several types of equipment to help pilots see and navigate in darkness. One such system is a thermal imaging system to help pilots locate targets. These systems sense heat from the ground and convert the heat into pictures. The hotter an object is, the brighter its image.

Attack helicopters also carry advanced visionics. These are electronics systems that help pilots see in all types of weather. Some systems include

FACT FILE

Helicopters to the Rescue

In the days before motorized vehicles, U.S. soldiers known as cavalry rode horses into battle. The cavalry had a reputation of riding to the rescue of foot soldiers. Today, helicopter pilots may be part of cavalry units. One such unit is the U.S. Army's 1st Squadron, 17th Cavalry Regiment serving in Iraq. The pilots spend most of their time flying across the countryside watching for trouble, or escorting convoys. But when a battle breaks out or a bomb goes off, the pilots fly in to the rescue.

AH-1 Cobras are the attack helicopters used by the U.S. ▲
Marines. This is a pair of AH-1W Super Cobras.

helmet-mounted displays, which project navigational information on the visor of the pilot's helmet. This includes altitude (how high the helicopter is flying), airspeed, and flight path. This way, the information is right in front of the pilot's eyes. Visionics systems can also find enemy locations and send that information to other aircraft or ground forces.

Attack helicopters are usually equipped with weapons towers. Each tower can include missiles, rockets, or machine guns. The missiles and rockets can pierce the armor on most armored vehicles, such as tanks, at a range of several thousand feet.

Chapter FOUR

Light Transport Helicopters

U.S. Air Force Staff Sergeant Kevin Stewart was one of four crew members aboard an HH-60G Pave Hawk helicopter on a mission in Afghanistan on the night of March 2, 2002. Their task was to fly with a second Pave Hawk to rescue three wounded U.S. soldiers from the battles of Operation Anaconda, where they had fought against Taliban soldiers. The Taliban was a religious group that had been in power in Afghanistan. The United States was at war with the Taliban because they would not turn over the people who had been responsible for the terrorist attacks on the United States on September 11, 2001.

As the pilot and co-pilot flew the aircraft, Stewart, the gunner, readied the machine gun in case of trouble. The crew used night vision goggles as they tried to locate the troops. They did not know exactly where they were going. They knew only the general location of the soldiers. The Pave Hawks sped along at just one hundred feet above the ground, hoping to spot the wounded men before Taliban soldiers found them.

At last Stewart spotted the soldiers and pointed out the area to the pilot. Bullets flew as opposing fighters shot at them. Stewart fired back at the opposing fighters using his helicopter's machine gun as both Pave Hawks landed. Stewart's return fire gave the U.S. soldiers enough time to get the wounded soldiers onto the helicopters.

As the Pave Hawk took off, the sky lit up with RPGs and tracer bullets.

As they took off, the sky lit up with RPGs and tracer bullets. These are special bullets containing a powder that burns bright red, so the gunner can see where the rounds are going. As Stewart fired back, the pilot decided on a quick route out of the area. Within fifteen minutes, they had the wounded men back at a U.S. air base. All three soldiers that they rescued survived.

Later, Stewart said that in the thick of the battle he had not even been aware of the intensity

FACTFILE

Black Hawk Hero

Captain Tammy Duckworth and her co-pilot, Chief Warrant Officer Dan Milberg, were returning from a routine mission over Iraq in their Black Hawk helicopter in November 2004. They skimmed along at 130 mph, barely ten feet above the ground.

Without warning, the bottom of Duckworth's helicopter exploded in flames as it was struck by a rocket-propelled grenade fired from the ground. The instrument panel went dark as the electrical system failed. Duckworth tried to use the rudder pedals on the floor to control the helicopter, but nothing worked. As she struggled for control of the aircraft, Milberg managed to guide the helicopter to the ground. As she reached up to turn off the rotors, Duckworth passed out.

Another Black Hawk landed nearby and its crew helped load the wounded, including Duckworth, on board. When she woke in the hospital later, Duckworth found out why she had not been able to work the rudder pedals. The explosion had ripped them away. The lower parts of her legs had also been lost.

In spite of her serious injuries, Duckworth was determined to continue serving her country. "For me to sit around and feel sorry for myself, that's going to dishonor my crewmates' efforts to save my life," she told reporters. Soon after the attack, she was promoted to major.

of the opposing fire. His main thought, he said, had been to do his job and ensure that his crew made it home safely.

For his actions that day, Staff Sergeant Kevin Stewart was awarded the Distinguished Flying Cross. He was humble about receiving the award. "This is a great honor," he said. "All the crew deserved this."

Transport Helicopters

The Pave Hawk and the similar Black Hawk are light transport helicopters. The Pave Hawk is used by the U.S. Air Force, while the Black Hawk is used by the U.S. Army. The two helicopters are the same model, but the Pave Hawk has more advanced communications, navigation, and weapons systems. Other transport helicopters include the CH53-D Sea Stallion, used by the U.S. Navy and Marines. The HH-60 Jayhawk, used by the Coast Guard, is a multipurpose helicopter that is often used for light transport, as well as interdiction and rescue.

A Pave Hawk can transport an eleven-person infantry squadron and all of its equipment. It can move the troops into or out of battle more quickly than ground vehicles can. Small transport helicopters can also carry a Howitzer, a type of cannon, and its six-member crew in a single flight.

Most small transport helicopters carry a crew of four. Roles of the crew members vary. The

Pave Hawk's crew, for example, consists of a pilot, co-pilot, flight engineer, and gunner. The pilot and co-pilot fly and navigate the helicopter. The flight engineer checks the aircraft before and after a flight, and takes care of any small problems during the flight. The gunner controls the weapons and fires back if the helicopter is under attack.

Light transport helicopters are often used in military rescue operations to move wounded soldiers to field hospitals. They may also fly as support during transport or rescue operations. They watch

▼ One of a Black Hawk's most important missions is to transport wounded soldiers. This soldier is being taken to a hospital in Iraq for treatment.

FACTFILE

Pave Hawk Fact Sheet

Primary use: Combat and search-and-rescue helicopter
Height: 16 feet, 8 inches
Length: 64 feet, 8 inches
Rotor diameter: 53 feet, 7 inches
Maximum speed: 184 mph
Crew: Pilot, co-pilot, flight engineer, gunner
Weapons: Two machine guns

out for and fire at opposing forces while other helicopters land to pick up equipment or soldiers.

Transport helicopters are often used in civilian rescue operations as well. The military may rescue people during natural disasters. Air ambulance companies use small transport helicopters to get injured people from the scene of an accident to a hospital quickly. Often they buy used military helicopters for this purpose.

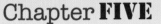

Chapter FIVE

Heavy Transport Helicopters

During Operation Desert Storm in 1991, several army lieutenants accidentally drove their Humvee off of a road and into quicksand. Trapped in the Humvee, they knew that it would sink into the loose, wet sand, and that they would eventually be buried. They radioed for help, but it was several days before anyone was able to come to their rescue. A crane could have pulled the Humvee and its crew free, but there were no cranes available. The only other way to free them was with a CH-47 Chinook helicopter.

By the time the Chinook's pilot, Chief Warrant Officer Glenn Bloom, and a crew chief arrived in their helicopter, the Humvee had sunk up to its windows in the quicksand. Bloom landed the Chinook in the quicksand, but kept the rotor spinning. This kept most of the weight of the helicopter off the quicksand and prevented the Chinook from rolling over and sinking as the Humvee had. Only the helicopter's wheels sank into the sand.

The crew chief jumped out of the helicopter with a sling held over his head. Though he quickly sank chest-deep into the sand, he worked his way over to attach the sling to the Humvee. It was hard work, and the operation took more than a half an hour. At

The helicopter lifted the 5,200-pound Humvee out of the quicksand and set it down on the road.

last the crew chief gave the signal that the Humvee was ready to be lifted from the sand.

But first Bloom had to lift the Chinook out of the quicksand. He carefully rocked the helicopter back and forth until he was able to pull out all of its wheels. Next, Bloom flew the Chinook over the top of the Humvee. The crew chief connected the helicopter's hook to the sling attached to the Humvee. Then, with the helicopter, Bloom lifted the Humvee out of the quicksand and set it down on the road. The Humvee weighed 5,200 pounds—almost three tons, or about the same as one and a half cars!

Bloom gave the grateful Humvee crew some food, picked up his crew chief, and flew back to base. The powerful Chinook had stepped outside of its usual role as a transport helicopter to take on a successful rescue mission.

Heavy Transport Helicopters

The Chinook is a heavy transport helicopter, used by the U.S. Army for carrying equipment, food, weapons, and troops. Though reporters sometimes describe it as slow and clumsy, the Chinook is actually very agile and capable of flying 184 mph, as fast as some attack helicopters.

▲ Marines replace one of the huge rotor blades on a CH-46E Sea Knight heavy transport helicopter.

FACTFILE

Sling Loading

Sling loading is a way for a transport helicopter to carry cargo outside of its cabin. Beneath the helicopter are three hooks. One is forward, or at the front of the helicopter, one is in the center, and one is aft, or at the rear.

The forward and aft hooks can carry loads of 17,000 pounds each. The center hook alone can carry loads as heavy as 26,000 pounds. That is similar to the weight of two medium-sized African elephants! The Chinook is so powerful that it can sling load and carry another 25,000-pound Chinook helicopter.

Other heavy transport helicopters include the CH-46 Sea Knight and the CH53-E Super Stallion, used by the U.S. Navy and Marines.

The Chinook is the helicopter that the U.S. Army relies on in its operations in Afghanistan. The average elevation or height of the Hindu Kush mountains, which cover most of Afghanistan, is almost nine thousand feet. The air at this elevation is thin. Helicopters with only a single horizontal rotor do not have enough air to push down and lift off the ground. Only the Chinook with its double rotors has enough power to lift in the thin atmosphere.

Heavy transport helicopters are large-bodied aircraft. The cabin of a Chinook, for example, holds forty-two cubic meters of cargo in an area of twenty-one square meters, a space large enough to hold two full-sized military Humvees. It has seating for thirty-three combat troops plus three crew members. In an emergency, up to twice as many troops can be carried, with some sitting on the floor in the aisles.

Since heavy transport helicopters are not generally used as attack aircraft, the weapons they carry are mostly for defense. They are usually armed with machine guns. They may also carry a missile approach warner, which lets the pilot know that a missile is approaching. A radar warner tells

FACT FILE

Chinook Fact Sheet

Primary use: Heavy transport helicopter
Height: 18 feet, 8 inches
Width: 15 feet, 9 inches
Length: 98 feet, 9 inches
Rotor diameter: 60 feet
Maximum speed: 184 mph
Crew members: Pilot, co-pilot, flight engineer

A U.S. Navy SH-60 Sea Hawk helicopter releases flares ▲ over the Pacific Ocean during an exercise.

the pilot that opposing forces are tracking the helicopter with radar and may be about to launch an attack. A jammer sends strong electronic signals to confuse the radar of opposing forces, making it harder for them to launch an attack.

Transport helicopters may also carry chaff and flare dispensers. These systems eject small pieces of metal foil, or chaff, as well as flares (flammable wands that can be ignited to give off light) from the helicopter. The chaff and flares attract radar guided or heat-seeking missiles so the weapons will explode harmlessly in the air, away from the helicopter. Chaff is also another way to confuse opposing radar.

Chapter SIX

Becoming a Military Helicopter Pilot

Training to become a military helicopter pilot takes hard work, practice, and dedication. All military pilots begin with the basics.

Different branches of the military have different flight training programs for pilots. For example, Aviator Training for the U.S. Navy and Coast Guard takes place at naval air stations in Florida, Mississippi, and Texas. Air Force bases in Texas, Oklahoma, and Georgia conduct joint training for Air Force and Naval pilots. The U.S. Army has a flight school in Alabama. Later, when students choose to specialize as helicopter pilots, those in the Navy, Marines, and Coast Guard will train together at a base in Florida.

While most programs require students to complete officer training before entering the flight program, the U.S. Air Force includes training for students who have not yet completed officer training. Each program differs in its details, but they all share a similar format.

Phase 1: Pre-flight Training

Phase 1 includes academic classes and pre-flight training. Before students get their hands on the controls of an aircraft, they must know how aircraft work. Students spend about six weeks in intense study, learning about engineering, aerodynamics (the forces that allow an aircraft to fly), navigation instruments (which help pilots find their way in the air), various aircraft systems, and survival skills. When they are not in front of a computer, working hard at computer-based lessons, students practice simulated parachute jumps from towers.

Phase 2: Flight Training

Phase 2, which lasts about twenty-two weeks (just under six months) is flight training. Regardless of what kind of aircraft the student pilots want to fly later, they all begin with computer-based flight simulators. After that, they actually fly for the first time, in a small airplane known as a trainer. With an instructor in the seat beside them, students learn the basics first: how to take off, fly, and land safely. They practice touch-and-go, in which instead of landing, they touch the wheels of their airplane to the runway and take right off again. This skill comes in handy in combat situations, where a pilot might

▼ An instructor (center) watches as two Air Force pilot students point out parts of an F-16 fighter jet.

attempt a landing, but suddenly come under attack and be forced to take off again.

After they master the basics, students learn some simple aerobatics, such as barrel rolls (rolling the aircraft in midair), and they learn to fly solo. They also learn to use the aircraft's instruments to help them navigate. Then students learn to fly in formation with other planes, and how to fly safely at low altitudes.

At the end of Phase 2, students decide what kind of pilot they would like to be. The choices include fighter or bomber pilot, tanker or airlift pilot, or helicopter pilot. Fighter planes attack other planes, as well as ground targets. Bombers drop bombs or missiles on ground targets. Tanker planes carry fuel for other aircraft. Airlift planes carry cargo and personnel.

Students may not always get the "track" they request. Those who earned the best scores on

Using a parachute is an ▲ important skill all pilots must learn. This airman practices his technique with a simulated jump.

written and in-flight tests during their training often get their first pick. Each track can take a certain number of students. If a track fills up, other students who wanted that track may have to choose another.

Phase 3: Advanced Aircraft Training

In the final phase, students learn to fly the aircraft that they will specialize in. They usually attend a school that specializes in a certain kind of aircraft. For helicopter pilots, the program involves about twenty-eight weeks of intensive training in flying helicopters.

Since helicopters work differently from airplanes, taking off, landing, and flying them require a new

▼ The T-6A Texan is a single-engine, two-seat trainer aircraft. Pilot trainees learn to fly these aircraft in Phase 2 of training.

FACT FILE

So You Want to Be a Military Helicopter Pilot?

Do you have what it takes? If you are a person who does not give up easily you have one of the most important qualities of a successful military pilot. A military helicopter pilot also has to be physically fit. Becoming physically fit and staying fit is a lifelong pursuit and can begin today. Pilots also have positive attitudes. They are "can-do" people. They must be resourceful and find ways to solve problems under stressful conditions.

Pilots in the military must also love adventure. There is no doubt that flying a helicopter in a war zone is thrilling, but there are responsibilities every pilot must face. Each mission must be completed to the best of the pilot's ability because other people's lives depend upon it.

set of skills. Students learn to use a helicopter's controls and instruments. They practice night flying and low-level flight. Graduates may then receive special training in a specific type of helicopter before they are finally assigned to a military unit as a pilot.

Outside of the Military

Once a helicopter pilot leaves the military there are many opportunities to continue flying helicopters.

Law enforcement is one career option for a military helicopter pilot. Police forces often need

FACTFILE

Medevac Missions

The term "medevac" is short for medical evacuation. It refers to an airplane or helicopter used as an ambulance. Helicopters are more commonly used because of their ability to easily take off from the scene of an accident and land in a relatively small space, such as the roof of a hospital.

Sometimes medevacs are called air ambulances. When people are seriously injured in traffic accidents, for example, they are airlifted to nearby trauma centers (hospitals which specialize in medical emergencies), where teams of doctors can work to save their lives. A medevac can get a person to a hospital far faster than an ambulance on the ground.

Medevacs were first developed during the Korean War (1950–1953) to help save soldiers' lives. The TV show M*A*S*H, popular in the 1970s, was based on the experiences of army surgeons and demonstrated how helicopters were used. The show was set during the Korean War. The name stands for Mobile Army Surgical Hospital.

helicopters to watch busy freeways and spot accidents and reckless drivers. Pilots may watch from the air when police on the ground move in to stop a crime, and follow any escaping suspects.

Air ambulance services need experienced pilots who can respond to emergencies. They may be called on to rescue injured people from the scene of a traffic accident, or from remote wilderness areas. Air ambulance pilots often have to fly in bad weather and in other dangerous conditions that military pilots have experienced.

Even Hollywood needs helicopter pilots. Movie studios often need them to make aerial photo flights in the filming of movies. They also need stunt pilots, who carry out dangerous stunts for action movies.

With the danger of combat behind them, former military helicopter pilots have the skills to succeed in any helicopter-related career. Most military helicopter pilots know how to operate their aircraft in difficult and dangerous conditions where lives and expensive equipment are at stake, and they know how to handle pressure. Useful in any career, whether involving helicopters or not, this knowledge stays with a pilot long after he or she leaves the military.

Air ambulance pilots often have to fly in bad weather and other dangerous conditions.

co-pilot—The second pilot in an aircraft, who assists the pilot and may take over if the pilot is injured.

crew chief—Helicopter crew member who takes care of and repairs the aircraft.

flight engineer—Helicopter crew member who inspects the helicopter before and after a flight and helps take care of it during a flight.

interdiction—Stopping the opposing side, such as smugglers or dangerous watercraft.

lift—The force that holds a helicopter or other aircraft in the air. It is caused by a downward flow of air off a helicopter's rotor or an airplane's wing.

machine gun—An automatic weapon that can fire many bullets rapidly.

missile—A rocket carrying explosive ammunition that may be launched by remote control.

navigate—To guide an aircraft along a planned route.

pilot—Helicopter crew member in charge of flying the aircraft.

radar—Tool that detects objects by sending out radio waves that bounce off of the objects.

rocket—An explosive weapon that is propelled by an engine.

rocket-propelled grenade (RPG)—A small rocket fired from a shoulder-mounted launcher, used against aircraft and tanks.

rotor— A set of blades on a helicopter that turn, producing the airflow that moves the aircraft forward and helps lift it into the air.

visionics—Electrical systems on a helicopter that enhance what a pilot is able to see in various conditions.

Books

Dartford, Michael. *Helicopters.* Minneapolis: Lerner Publishing Group, 2003.

Doeden, Matt, and Gail Saunders-Smith. *Military Helicopters.* Mankato, Minn.: Capstone Press, 2005.

Green, Michael, and Gladys Green. *Weapons Carrier Helicopters: The UH-60 Black Hawks.* Mankato, Minn.: Capstone Press, 2005.

Hansen, Ole Steen. *Helicopters.* New York: Crabtree Publishing, 2004.

Holden, Henry M. *Black Hawk Helicopter.* Berkeley Heights, N.J.: Enslow Publishers, Inc., 2001.

Holden, Henry M. *Rescue Helicopters and Aircraft.* Berkeley Heights, N.J.: Enslow Publishers, Inc., 2002.

Internet Addresses

http://www.army.mil
   The U.S. Army Web site

http://www.uscg.mil
   The U.S. Coast Guard Web site

http://www.usmc.mil
   The U.S. Marine Corps Web site

INDEX